# Life in Ink

© 2010 by Kenneth Peele III. All rights reserved

Life in Ink/ by Kenneth Peele III

ISBN  1450596592

EAN-13  9781450596596.

In loving memory of

~ Kenneth Peele Sr. ~

# Life in Ink

### Kenneth Peele III

A Red Ink Production

# Contents

Preface- 7

## I.

My Mirror Shattered- 11

Life in Ink- 12

A Plea to End Disbelief- 13

Diary Excerpt from a Child's Mind- 14

Miami 12-25-96 16

## II.

Homeless- 21

Medicine Man- 22

The Young Father Cycle-          23

College Philosophy-              24

Why My Uncle Doesn't Fly-        26

## III.

My Sweet Breakfast-              29

If Eyebrows were Umbrellas-      30

While Wrapped in My Test-        31

Even on My Bad Day-              32

Ode to my Swan-                  33

Bright Light-                    34

In Your Arms-                    35

My Petal from Afar-              36

| | |
|---|---|
| Black and White- | 37 |
| I Hope that you think of me- | 38 |
| Bed- | 39 |

## IV.

| | |
|---|---|
| Annual- | 43 |
| Eireen- | 44 |
| Why I don't Mind Stares- | 46 |
| The End of Romance- | 47 |
| Black Globe- | 48 |
| Anticipation- | 49 |
| The Theory of Socialization- | 50 |
| Homage- | 51 |

## V.

When all we do is Argue-          55

A Penny Worth of Hope-          56

A Butterfly in Bay County-       57

A Skater's Deployment-           58

Modern Warfare-                  59


Acknowledgements-                61

# Preface

The Rorschach Test is an assessment using inkblot pictures to diagnose personality structure. By using an individual's feedback on inkblots, the test's administrator will be able to ascertain an understanding of a person's thought process, and the way they view the world. I feel that one's personality helps to define their life, and how enjoyable that life may be. Therefore, this book is my personality in writing, which references my *life in ink*.

*I*

## My mirror shattered

But before that I saw a little black boy

with hair like small raisins attached on every end.

He balled his fist, and dried his right eye

while his other hand became a Bounty towel

absorbing puddles on his round dimples

like when his mom would wipe droplets

off freshly washed plums.

# Life in Ink

Born covered in red blood, which against my skin looks crimson.

Then cleaned and given to my parents who will raise me, dedicate me

to God, and surround me with a family that embodies blood's viscosity.


I grew in a world where the devil's trials have left me blue

singing BB songs, and forcing air through a rusted harmonica

until my face looks indigo and my cheeks start to burn from stretching.


Invictus resounds in my ears, reminding me of the black night

whose darkness test my mind. Yet, I remain unconquered, and shall be

until my soul escapes my body, and my thoughts live on in ink.

# A Plea to End Disbelief

Hope like a hot air balloon rises,

toting our child like ideas and flights of fancy.

We seek help by taking loans, begging family,

and convincing others to believe in our dreams.

Then at some point people realize

that our aspirations lack true merit.

Those people then prosecute us

for the ideas we believed would soar

like that hot air balloon.

# Diary Excerpt from a Child's Mind

I woke expecting to be bothered by my Mickey Mouse clock.

Instead I got an eerie feeling blanketed by silence.

My transformers weren't littered on the ground.

The carpet looked clean like my dad after shaving.

The frame near the bed held a boy's portrait.

He was familiar, but he wasn't me.

Fear entered like the Foot Clan in my head with all their ninja stealth

while my eyes became my mother's dripping shower head.

Mustering the courage of Donatello,

I left the strange bed and smeared my tears.

The icy feel of tile chilled my bare feet.

Blank hallways gave no answers to my whereabouts.

My frustration was illustrated on my dark plum cheeks.

Hope lost like my mother's keys.


A woman with a mouse's voice said my name.

My godmother appeared behind me

saying "your mother had a baby girl last night"

## Miami 12-25-97

No snow or cold weather, only palm trees

        that whisper as a cool breeze

        causes leaves to belly dance.


You wake up early, clawing at wrapping paper

        like raptors who throw

        red wads of crinkled paper.


Hug your mom and dad, and thank them

        for the Nintendo that you

        plan to play Mario on later.


While you connect the game to your TV,

        the aroma of cheese grits waltzes

        from the kitchen to your bedroom


You eat a light breakfast saving room

        for the Christmas buffet of glazed ham,

pigeon peas and rice, and collard greens

among other dishes prepared by your Grandma

whose food seems as well seasoned

as her sixty six years.

Later you ride with your parents to your

grandparents house, where you hear laughter

seeping through its pores as you pull up.

Then enter to be greeted by pinched cheeks, hugs,

pats on the back, and at least ten people who say

you're getting to be tall like your poppa.

Then you and your cousins go outside to knock

on your friends door and find someone

with a football for a shirts vs. skins game

since the weather is practically room temperature,

and the last gift you want is the chance

to mimic Deon's last end zone dance.

*II*

# Homeless

Johnny Boy lost

his money,

his house,

and his honey.

He roams the streets

dragging his feet

in shoes like

worn dish rags.

Ash colored

hands cupped

wishing for charity

as town folks

pass him by

donating sny remarks,

and pitiless hearts.

# Medicine Man

### for Johnny Boy's Momma

He was located conveniently close to my dwelling, making it easy
        for the young and old villagers to frequent his house.
My mother was a patient of his for many moons,
        transporting satchels with his medicine to our home daily.
After the prescription, her eyes were glossy like fresh salmon pupils.
        Her mouth would hang agape, but her mind rested peacefully.
In old age my mother still yearned for the medicine's calming power.
        A double inhale causing visions of her former deer dancer.


There's a new medicine man now though, they say he's a doctor
        making house calls to give my mother personal treatment.
He uses a spoon to boil his potion, then siphons it through a syringe
        squeezing out a drop to make sure the needle works.
He removes his leather belt, using it to strangle my mother's arm
        as veins seem to crawl beneath her skin.
The needle stabs the worm-like vein sending tremors through her body
        until the potion gives her rest.

# The Young Father Cycle

I was only seven when

My father worked from 10 till 10,

Off too late to buy a tree.

Instead of Power Rangers for Christmas

He gave me, his crave for money.


I used to be the fat kid

Asking Momma for a bologna sandwich

Now I struggle to buy Gerber.


No more father and son fishing trips

My child-hood robbed by a man,

Who under his black ski mask was green as Benjamin.

Now 10 years 9 months later, I will give this gift again.

# College Philosophy

There's a fortune cookie at the bottom

    of every bottle

        Maybe 2

If you chug, drink quickly, or shotgun till

    your head starts to throb

        prophecies spill out

Providing more info than what I should've learned

    from the psyche books in

        PSY 1100

Or a lack luster professor whose hair is the color

    of soap scum

        on a Dial bar

and with a voice like the public advisory

      for a tornado warning

          minus the harsh beep tone.

I prefer the advice of the old guy who still

      goes to frat parties and shouts

          "Don't let school

                get in the way of college"

# Why My Uncle Doesn't Fly

Uncle Bobby on his reclining throne

watches birds through the windowsill.

He still lives in his mother's home

whose support makes him ill.

He sees a red cardinal in the tree,

avoiding what appears to be

annoying rain drops

the sound of lima beans in a pot.

Bobby eats the same damn Gwartney franks

served with leftover Walmart wild rice

for almost a month, *No thanks*.

Do personal standards change with price?

Then Bobby watches the red exemplar bird

think of pride, and gather its remaining nerve

flying through the deadly tempest

against a dreary day that seems relentless.

*III*

# My Sweet Breakfast

My family and I sat at the oaken dining table

to eat our morning waffles.

I slowly poured the Aunt Jemima syrup.

It was thick, sticky,

and the color of my girlfriend's skin.


After gawking at the beautiful dish

I bit into the waffles grid-like cerebellum.

The warm and soggy bits

were like socks after walking home in the rain

with my girlfriend,

who told countless stories with no point.

She wasn't as sweet as her appearance,

like the light syrup I used by accident.

## If eyebrows were umbrellas

I would stare into your pupils

without fret of clouds around me.

You'd smile and a gust of wind would

blow from underneath the umbrella

to propel me upward, above clouds

to a realm where sunshine reigns

and only thoughts of you shroud my mind.

## While wrapped in my test

All the numbers blended into Matrix like patterns,

my eyes changed focus from that Algebra test

to your flea market manicured toes.

Then I stared at your dancers feet, set free in Payless thongs,

the ballerina in lace that would never know my feelings,

who sat at her desk playing a guessing game with equations.

I tore a portion of my scrap paper off,

then used a make shift calligraphy to write my name and number

hoping it wouldn't remind you of a third grade

check No or Yes letter, and slid it your way.

Then Mrs. Cather snatched the note,

and scribbled a red F on my test.

But at least I made you smile.

## Even on my bad day

I look forward to rain showers

in hope that we could share my umbrella.

A black blanket drawing me closer to your body's warmth

welcoming cold drops, and wet socks for a chance to get close to you.

I picture one hand interlocked with yours while the other keeps us dry,

protecting your dark chocolate skin from the elements.

As we walk my mind remains focused on your lips,

 like honey soaked pillows

while I unconsciously walk through puddles

that appear dry in comparison.

The gloss from your lips like the sun after a shower, its reflection

turning rain drops into a prism that forms rainbows after bad weather.

## Ode to My Swan

You are both beautiful and valiant.

In the midst of rain, I watch your wings flutter as you fling droplets.

A resilience only matched by your extrinsic radiance.

I long to simply caress your wing, but you fly when I draw near.

Pause my swan, I mean no harm. I simply admire all that you are.

Majestic in appearance, your subtle beauty has made me a bird watcher,

with my binoculars focused only on you.

Then my unexpected words spark your depart

Your long neck and wings stretched fully in mid-flight,

when all I ask is that you trust and relax.

Where we are will be our safe haven.

# Bright Light

When a glare hits the ocean locking a captain's stare
        causing ship wrecks and bits of wood to fly.

I know the sea has mirrored your radiance
        as glimmers dance across waves.

Those men lured to you by that seductive light
        like the Siren's call which seals a sailors fate.


Though your eyes like a beacon will guide me
        even amidst clouds and treacherous storms.

I pursue my light house until I reach stable ground,
        with my course directed by more than sight.

My focus is on what you are, and my path
        to safer shores.

# In Your Arms

I wake in a plush bed of budding carnations

with the sun's faint glare kissing my cheek.

The dew from last night's fantasies

lightly glaze my skin, reminiscent of

the glare from fresh-water salmon scales.

I dream of my finger tips grazing your pores,

the shiver it sends through your body

like the subtle breeze in early March.

I know that we will grow, since spring is near.

Our carnation buds will flourish soon.

# My Petal from Afar

People always admired your beauty, including me,

    but I imagined your scent as unpleasant.

How could something as beautiful as you are

    have a smell that matches perfectly?

Are other flowers jealous of you, or

    do they despise God for creating perfection?

I dare not draw near for fear of thorns,

    but I admire you from a distance.

Since this change in seasons I fear I am too late,

    and have missed the chance to sniff my rose.

## Black and White

My feelings for you are too complicated for a simple

white pad and black ink. I need a movie.

I miss the caress of your full moon lips

reminiscent of el fin in Casa Blanca.

Me giving you that final hug, wrapping my arms

around you, the way thoughts of you shroud my mind.

I long for your embrace and dread your absence,

left with a single strand of your hair clinging

on my collar, flaunting its floral scent,

with that strand and memories being the sole

souvenirs of your presence as I watch your train depart.

## I hope that you think of me

At least dream the dreams that I do

with visuals of me and you hands intertwined

as we sip wine in front of a wicker basket

filled with homemade dishes, and that basket wishes

it could mimic the way our fingers interlock

while we sit without shoes or socks

allowing sand to grace our feet, whose soles

cling to those cool grains of this tropical dessert in Fall.


All while I stare at your lips and think of their caress.

A kiss with the taste of honey, a high like euphoria,

And the feel you want more of. Like falling into plush pillows.

Then I wake from my dream in the crux of total bliss,

with you giggling at my slow blinks, and I laugh and think,

or at least hope that you feel the same way about me.

# Bed

With hair like black silk, I can imagine

a peaceful sleep caressing your smooth sheets,

staring into your eyes like crystal balls

which display our future together.

I kiss your memory foam lips, taking me

to youthful memories like playing in the park.

A giddy time filled with games of tickle fight

that made me squirm and laugh, but now

I have graduated to gentle kisses on the crease

between your neck and chin that make you contort

then shiver followed by moans of ecstasy.

So I move closer to your body to hold you

and quench my desire while setting my hands ablaze.

*IV*

# Annual

We jump from Spring to Winter, bud then die

while I dream of blooms with the sweet fragrance

of pollen dancing on all your petals.

The special memories we shared on a repeating reel,

with Hamilton's *Point of it All* playing in the background.

I drown my hopes or quench them with dismissed

wishes squandered plucking petal by petal

in my flower piano recital with one of two chords

bored into my head until I change songs or

turn this into a perennial.

# Eireen

Walking in here with that sexy sequined dress

the color of blazing sirens,

pounding even the tap dance of her sultry twist.

I hear the screams from male hearts,

trampled like the boy crossing the street

who didn't see the fire engine coming.

The frayed ends of her cocktail dress

made from the extracted lashes of admirers

who watch the clit-tat her stilettos make.

Similar to her other admirer's,

I'm lost in Eireen's Victoria Secret perfume,

invigorated by her coffee colored skin

causing me to day dream on my way to work.

Then the addicting/hot libation spills,

permanently burning the crotch of my pants.

# Why I Don't Mind Stares

When you leave the withdrawal sets in.
I miss holding you at night, creating warmth
like sipping warm cocoa near the fireplace.

Even a subtle touch from you
is a breeze which blows out that fire,
sends chills, and fosters goose bumps.

Then I lick my lips with hope that nectar
from one of your sweet kisses lingers
unexpectedly like a leftover morsel of chocolate
from one of the smores I used to make.

Now I fiend for one more smore,
a delicious treat reminiscent of our
bodies whenever I hold you,
like chocolate on your marshmallow skin.

# The End of Romance

I stare at you on this dark night

as Luna's pale light kisses your cheek

the way I desperately need to

express on your grape colored lips,

but you lie there with a stoic stare,

stiff and motionless. Your once light skin

now with a starch colored complexion.

I prop your head and tangled hair,

then exert pressure on your chest

followed by our failed exchange of oxygen.

# Black Globe

The sun looks blue, it blends with the sky.

The stars are black, they match the night.

Lately my dreams have been my torture

as if I sleep in the inquisition's strappado.

My nightmares are in search of an oracle.


I have watched your once bright eyes

covered by the cloak of your eye lids.

Your meager mannequin corpse

dressed in a cocoon of stiff flesh.

Sleep peacefully in your porcelain bed.

Saying goodbye is still impossible,

so your dust will linger on my mantle.

# Anticipation

I dream like I want to die,

    or at least never wake up

when thoughts of you tuck me in

    like I'm trapped under sheets,

as if housekeeping made-up my bed

    with me still in it.


The thought of your arrival turns my

    apartment into a Four Seasons suite.

Plan on comp. room service from me

    with breakfast in bed,

and deep tissue massages

    running from your neck down to your legs.

# The Theory of Socialization

I dream a world with people, faces removed.

They interact in silence without smiles or expressions,

Only granite grins on stoic heads.

Though there is peace now with the faceless.

They do not argue, bicker, or kiss.

No more moist pillows that when compressed

form lips whose puckered embrace sends chills.

They're all the same, so war has no motive.

Only unison reigns amongst an army of clones

who impose no harm or delight on one another.

They are trapped in a society of boredom, yet

because they have never known, they cannot dream

of even a kiss.

# Homage

Adieu-

This is goodbye,

farewell,

the cupped

rotating hand

from Ms. America

as I end my personal

practice of reverence

to mock idols

and celebrities.


Are you so different

than me?

Your expertise

at your craft

grants success,

but palms sweating,

and loss of speech

in your presence

is not due.


I chose to save

my respect

for those with power.

The men and women

who can affect change.

The Obama's, Gandhi's,

and political leaders

who serve as

protectors of peace.

They deserve my homage.

*V*

# When all we do is Argue

If beauty lies in the eye of the beholder,

then the environment would have my eyes tear ridden.

Officials bicker in debates allowing issues to smolder

like a volcano on a distant island hidden

amidst trees and foliage which were once veils

that are now withdrawn thanks to toxic emissions

which kill trees and birth a greenhouse eruption of hell.

With little remorse except for guilty admissions

from politicians who fear causing tension.

# A Penny Worth of Hope

After school days

that seemed longer than miles

I remember flicking pennies high

then watching them plummet

into the wishing fountain at the mall.


I used to wish for that 87' red Benz in the classifieds,

I used to wish for a date with my cute lab partner

Chardea from Physics,

but never thought to wish for life back then,


Until I witnessed the people at the twin towers beg for it.

Visions of flesh made pennies

occupied my mind like unwanted houseguests

while other New Yorkers missed their loved ones.


Flicking pennies into a shopping mall fountain is pointless,

when all you see are bodies diving toward gray pavement.

# A Butterfly in Bay County

### for Martin Lee Anderson

From my driver's seat I see black bodies with orange wings fade to
> brown decorated with large black dots.

Swarms of them flying with the traffic current, trying to keep up with
> the speeding hunks of metal in Panama City

which take pauses at stoplights, like a robotic routine, to ensure the
> maximum efficiency of the traffic system in place by the
> government.


Then at the light, one creature gets tired of keeping up with the traffic,
> and lands on my window

immediately punched and kicked around by the same prejudice wind
> that helps to propel my aerodynamic car.

Then eventually the Butterfly is killed

> *- it shouldn't have landed on my window,*

> and no one cares because there's still more in the swarm.

Plus, it's just a butterfly.

# A Skater's Deployment

**for our troops**

We all form a single file line to approach the counter

shout our size, then wait for the wrinkled guy with a limp

to find a 6 that with his blurred vision ends up as a 9.

I lace up my skates then begin to move dodging a barrage of youth

who have yet to master the art of avoiding people.

How can one identify the type of youth that skates absent of fear,

who has no concept of danger and skates blindly without caution?

I know I am not perfect. I still need to master stopping,

though I know when to slow down, and reduce my speed

before my destination. Therefore I can't stop immediately

and choose a gradual withdrawal.

# Modern Warfare

These days our ways have changed, wars still

take place on a battlefield, but the real battles

take place in our homes.

I doubt an action like Hiroshima will be repeated,

but the media can drop a bomb on American homes

alerting us of the fact that a prominent black man

can get arrested in his home with proper ID shown.

# Acknowledgements

Creating this book has been an arduous task, although its completion has been one of my most rewarding accomplishments thanks to God who gives me strength.

For your continued love and support, thank you to my family, friends, loved ones, and especially my mother and father whose upbringing has molded the person that I am.

Thank you to the Florida State University Creative Writing Department in Tallahassee, Florida for honing my literary talents. In addition, thank you to Dorene Martin, Chelsea Peele, Abayomi Bamiro, and all the members of Red Ink Press for helping to edit this book's manuscript.

Additionally, much credit is due to the individuals who have helped to inspire many of my poems: A. Mann, C. Murray, S. Johnson, C. Barron, J Tate, and F. Nattiel.

Finally, to Ryan A. Fletcher, thank you for your review and overall contribution to *Life in Ink*.